PHARMACY TECH

COLORING BOOK

THIS BOOK BELONGS TO:

____

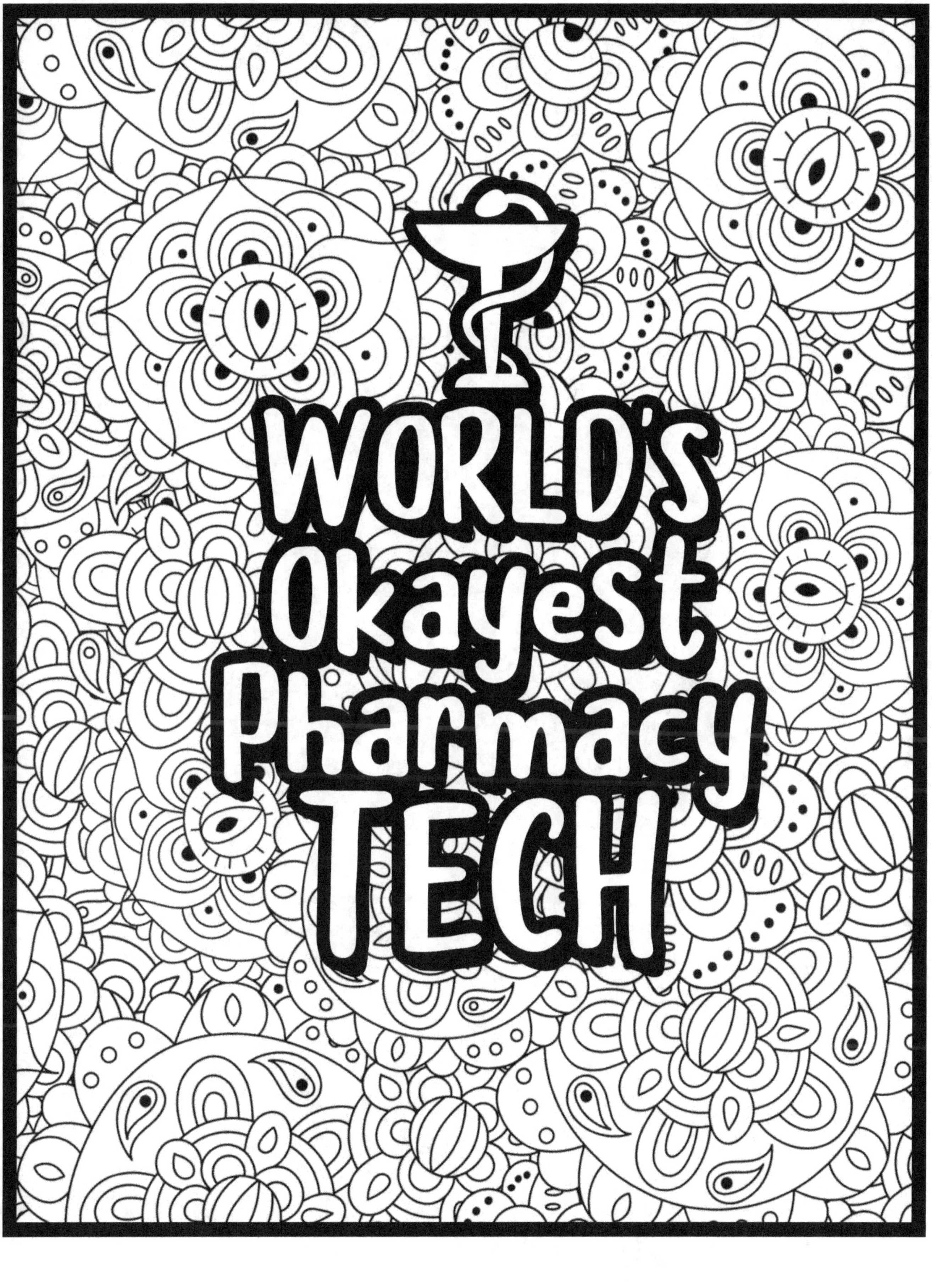
WORLD'S
Okayest
Pharmacy
TECH

PHARMACY
TECH.
HEALER.
LEGEND.

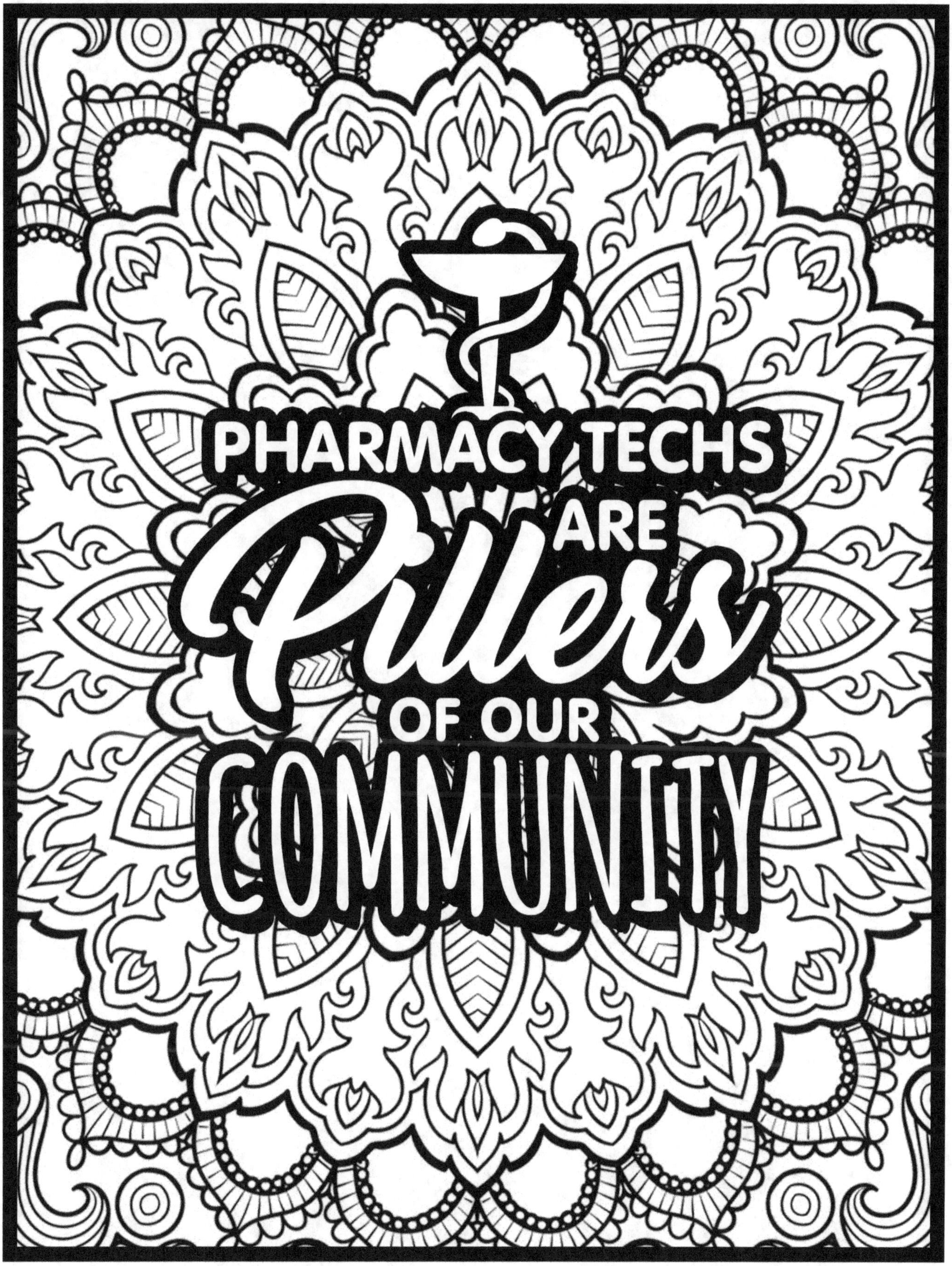
PHARMACY TECHS
ARE
Pillers
OF OUR
COMMUNITY

I SUFFER
FROM
RESTING
PHARMACY
TECH
FACE

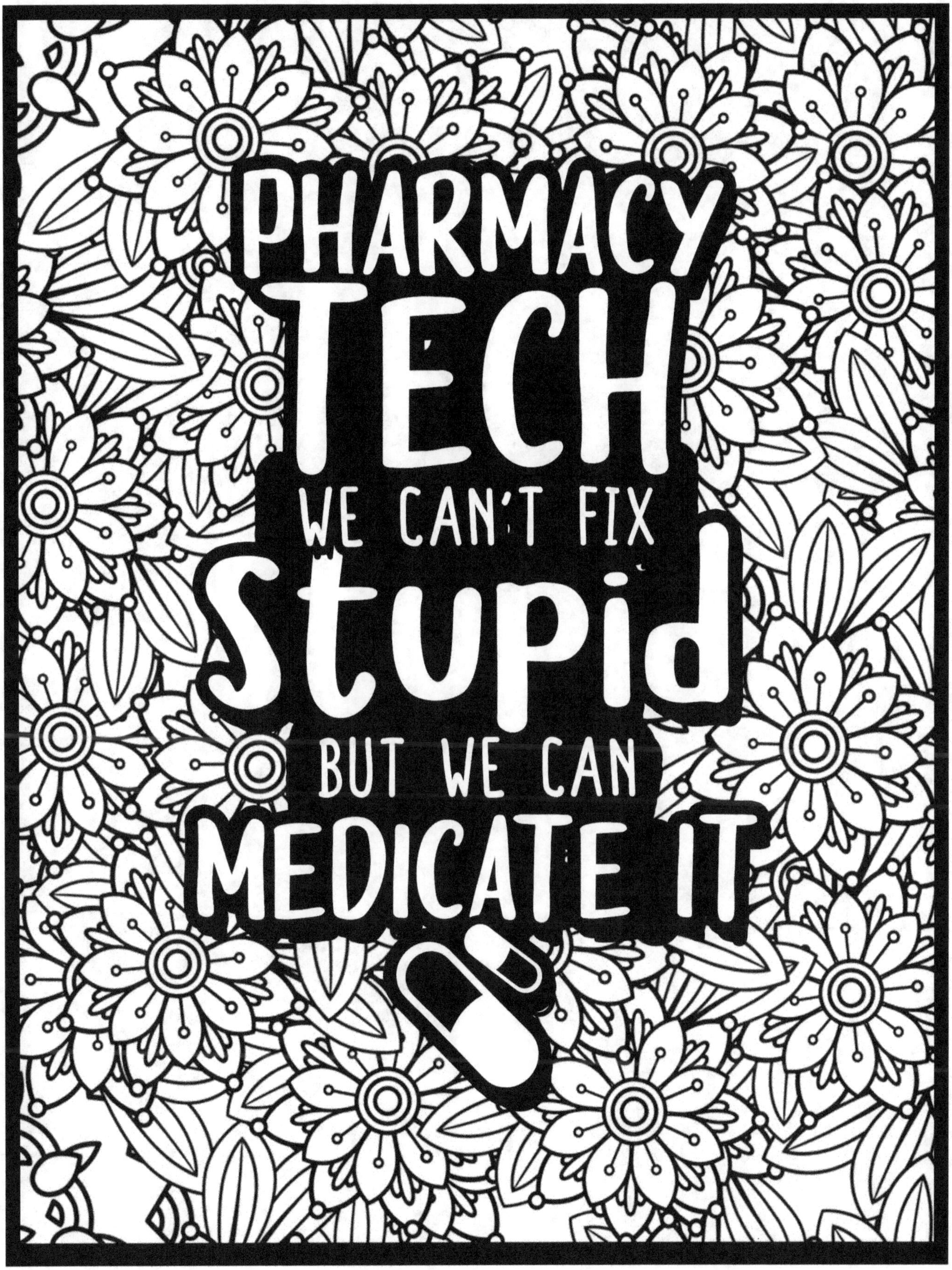
PHARMACY
TECH
WE CAN'T FIX
Stupid
BUT WE CAN
MEDICATE IT

I'M A
Pharmacy
TECH
WHAT'S YOUR
SUPER
POWER?

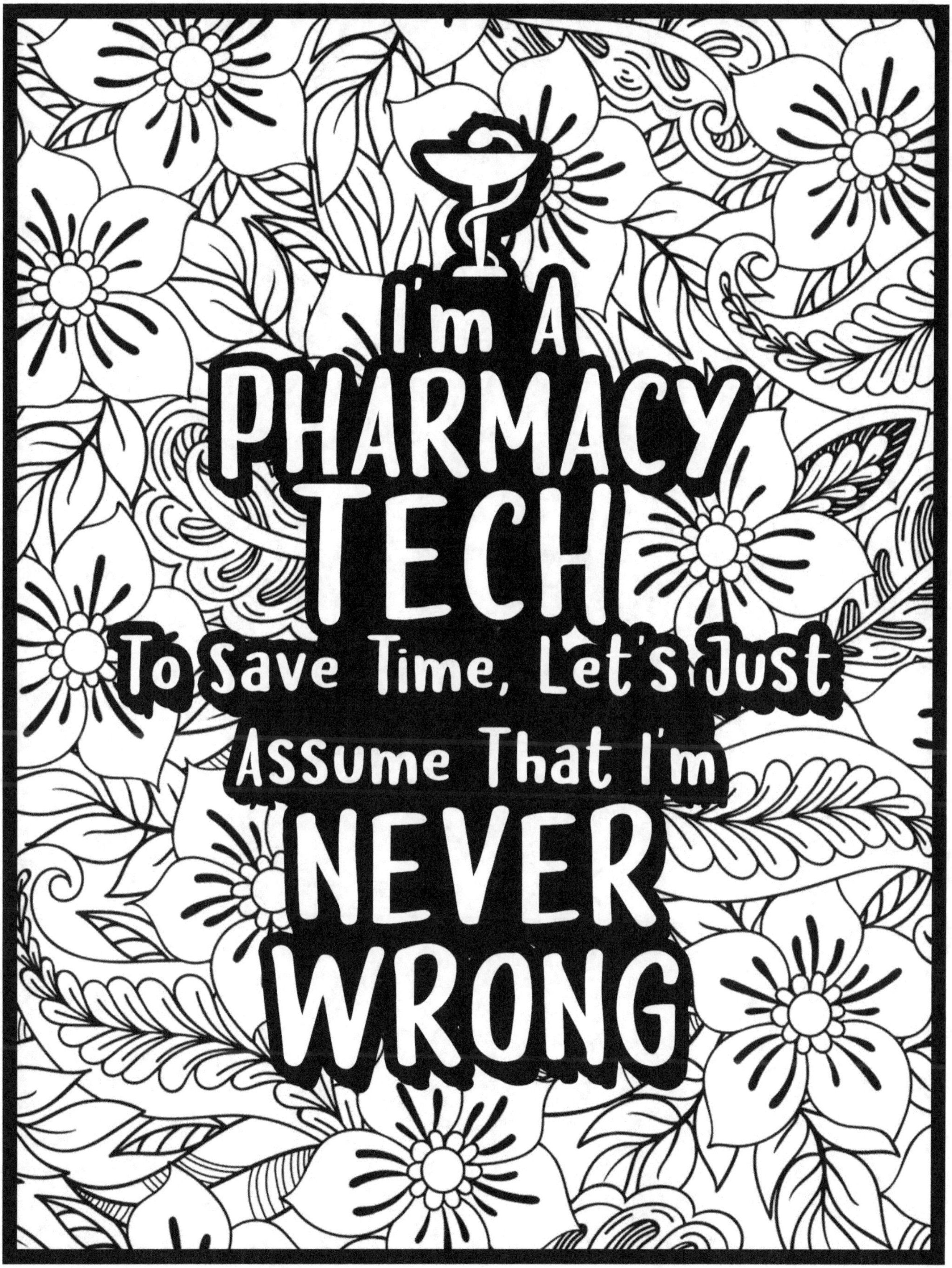
I'm A
PHARMACY
TECH
To Save Time, Let's Just
Assume That I'm
NEVER
WRONG

What
the
Actual
FUCK
?

It's What it
Fucking
is

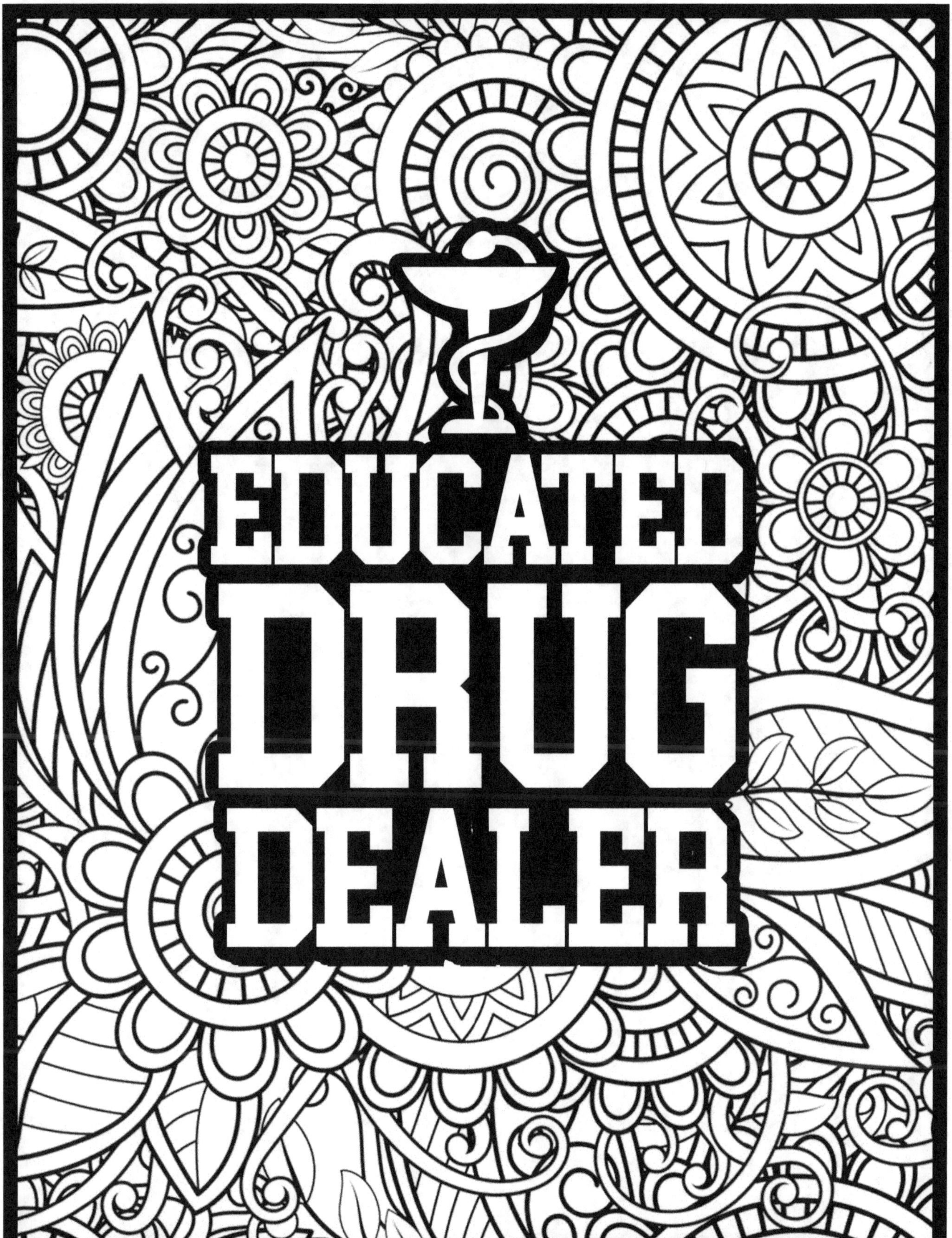
EDUCATED
DRUG
DEALER

GOOD MORNING
DOCTOR
UNFORTUNATELY
WE DON'T HAVE
SCRIBBLE
IN STOCK

STAYS LATE
TO FILL Rx
PATIENT
WENT
SHOPPING

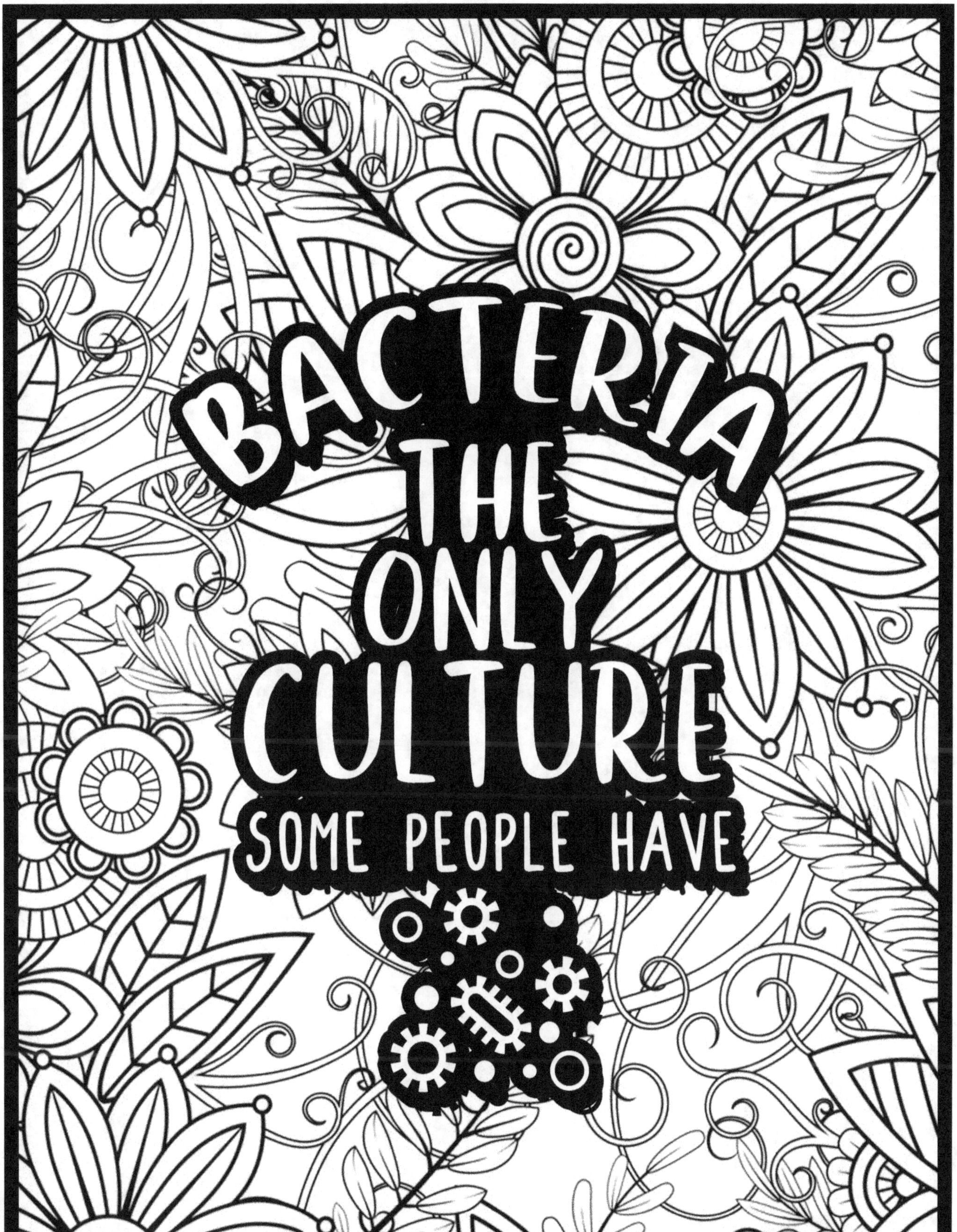
BACTERIA
THE
ONLY
CULTURE
SOME PEOPLE HAVE

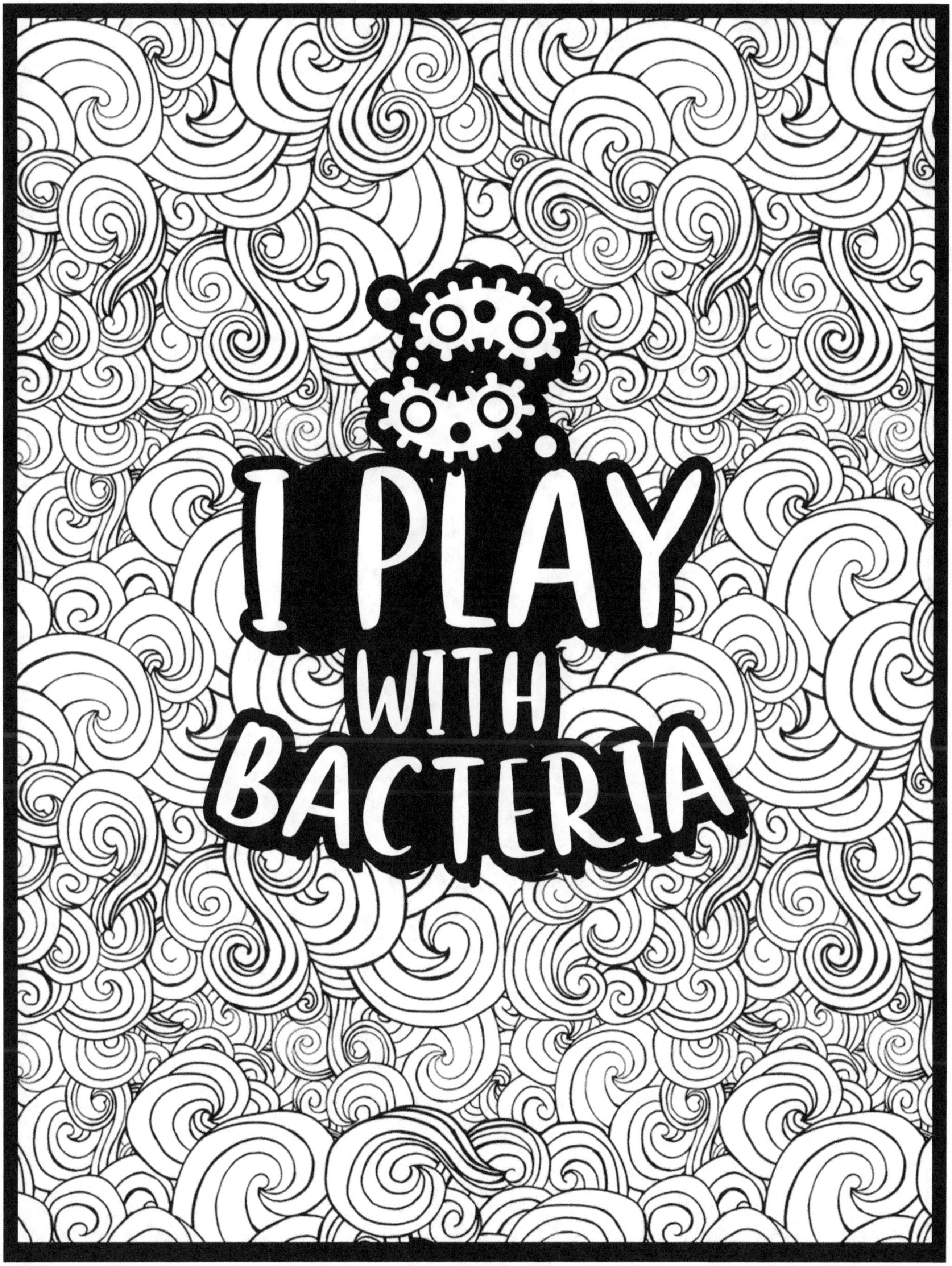
I PLAY
WITH
BACTERIA

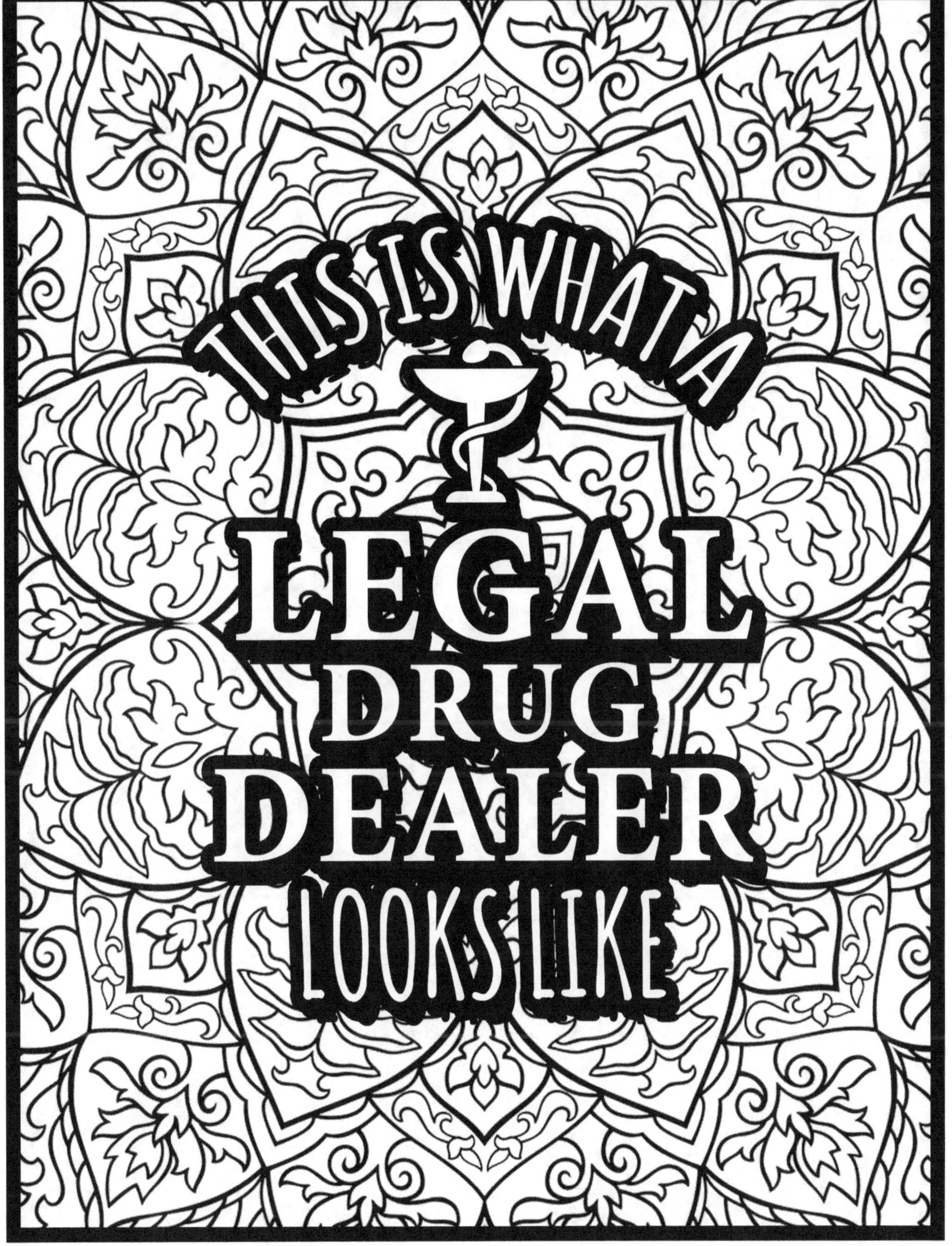
THIS IS WHAT A
LEGAL
DRUG
DEALER
LOOKS LIKE

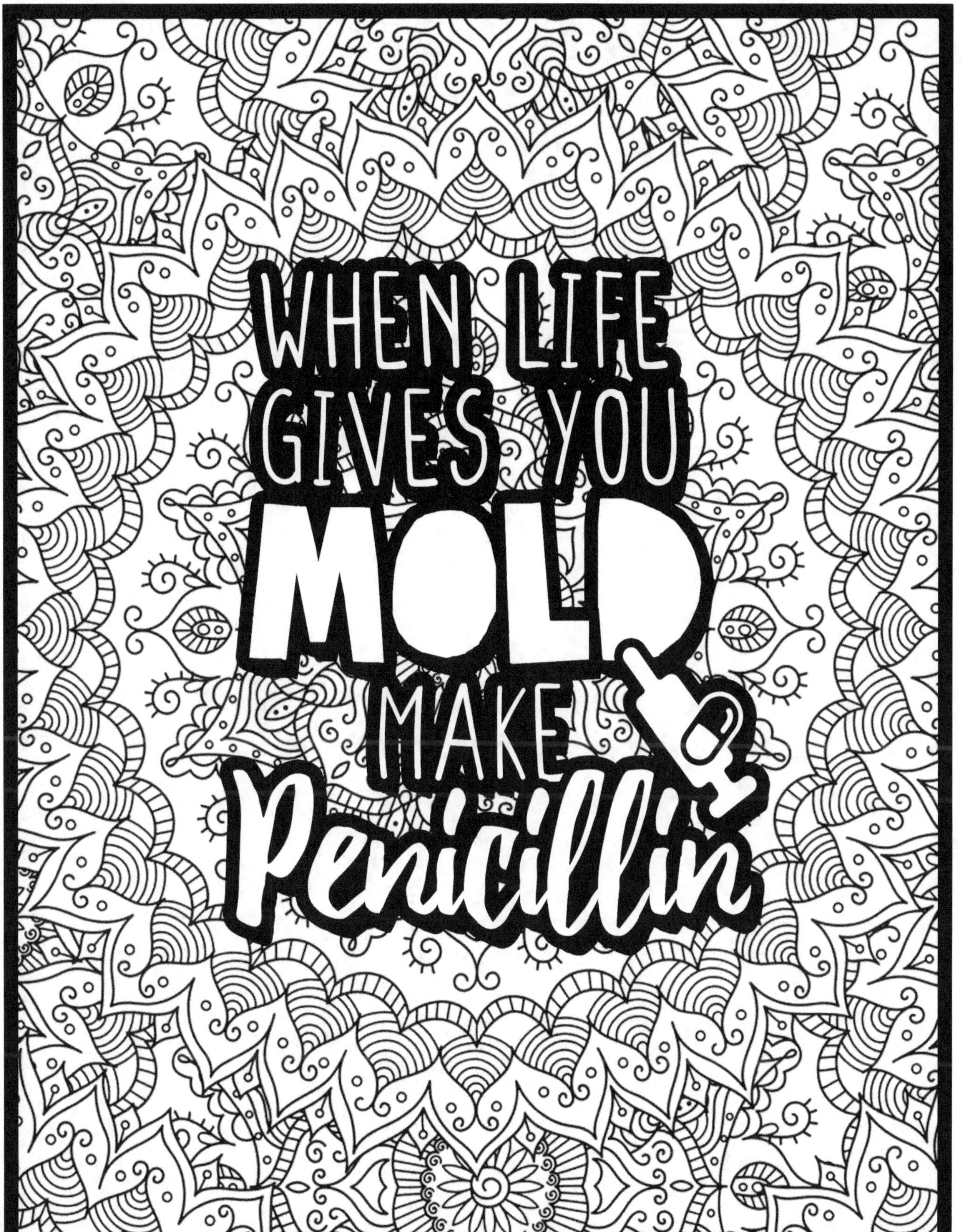
WHEN LIFE
GIVES YOU
MOLD
MAKE
Penicillin

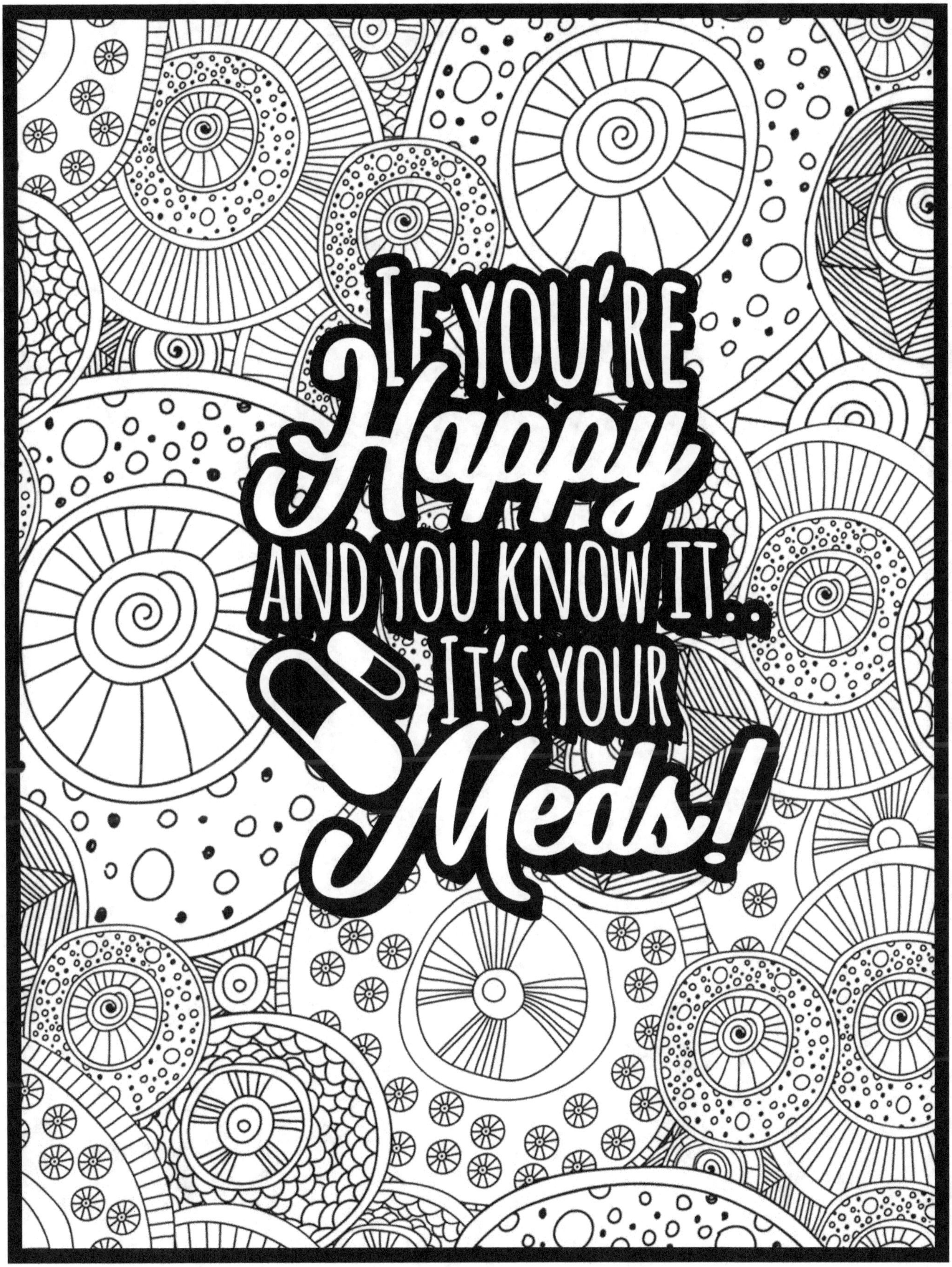
If you're
Happy
and you know it...
It's your
Meds!

LET THAT SH!T Go!

IF I DON'T
MOVE FAST
PEOPLE WILL HAVE THE
CHANCE
TO ASK ME THINGS!

ABSOLUTELY
F*CKING

www.ingramcontent.com/pod-product-compliance
Lightning Source LLC
Chambersburg PA
CBHW080628220526
45467CB00011B/3413
* 9 7 9 8 6 9 6 9 4 3 9 1 6 *